GW00776033

The Cradle of The Game

England & Scotland, Wales & Ireland

by Stuart Roy Clarke

Book Sponsored by

Derry City 'Steps out of Brandywell' 2005

In and out of membership of the United Kingdom clutch of grounds.

Photographs & Texts by Stuart Roy Clarke

"Stuart Clarke, in my opinion, is the finest football photographer in this country with his ability to capture the heart and soul of the game from its grass roots and the parks to the highest professional level. His ability to illustrate the love and emotion for the game, its excitement, its triumphs and tragedies in picture form of both participants and above all spectators is unsurpassed. Football of course is very much part of the fabric of our social life and Stuart's photographs illustrate that fabric in the finest quality."

Gordon Taylor, Chief Executive, Professional Footballers Association

MILLWALL 'VIEWING THE SNOWY DEN' 1991

The old bit of land is cleared…revealing…an ancient burial ground…the football pitch!

Introduction

More than 2 decades ago I began *The Homes of Football* believing myself to have a mission in showing the changing face of football, after the recent Hillsborough tragedy and the subsequent Lord Justice Taylor Report. I believed I was in the right place at the right time to account for THE most interesting period of football-history since records began; a national institution in BIG trouble was, crucially, reinventing itself. And it was something I had a natural affinity for, so I set about recording it, showing the game old and new, intertwined, again and again and again so that it all felt connected.

I never deserted that lamp, but the mission slightly dimmed as the years rolled on…

Then 20 years later there came, rather than a token anniversary, a real sense of mission again, to start telling the story once more, this time as **The Cradle of The Game**. If the threat to professional football had before been about negligence, disquiet, falling attendances…the threat now would be expressed in financial & ownership issues; football's popularity bubble (growing attendances across the board) had certainly not burst. My response as a photographer would be to show the values at the heart of the game, as well as you can do in photographs and a few words.

The Fans response meanwhile is to seize the day and seize the club: *we won't wait on a knight in shining armour to come save the club in the hour of need. It shouldn't come to this. And It won't again.*

The ideal, quite achievable, is all clubs be owned with a majority share (51%) by the fans; private investment is welcome to make up the rest (49%). Why have a club bear the name of a town if it has little to do with it!

Ironically, as I write, we could all end up owning Liverpool FC after the bank that loaned it monies is itself bailed out by the nation!

This 'Cradle' book is about the amazing clutch of clubs we have in this country. All four home countries are given title deeds because they have each and all played a part in where we have got to. How could we ignore George Best. Or Celtic & Rangers and the stream of great Scottish managers south? Wales recently reinvigorated The FA Cup and The Play-Offs by staging these key matches in Cardiff, in a beautiful city centre, et cetera.

Of course the English Premier League is the single biggest driver in football anywhere in modern times and a source of great pride the World over; it is hard to see the PL star fading…but is it an *English League*? Historically: yes. It came to prominence quickly, yet one could claim it was decades in the making and owes its roots to the British football empire. The Premier League then is the Jerusalem of William Blake's *green & pleasant land…*

Here's to park football and to Non-League Football, to League Football, to Premier League Football which make up 'the pyramid' of leagues we have here in England and an achievement to rival anything in Egypt.

HUDDERSFIELD TOWN 'LEEDS ROAD AT TWILIGHT' 1993

The old ground nestled amongst streets and factories, as seen from Kinder Bank. Jay and his Dad are down there somewhere. Walking their walk to a kind of work – together - to watch the football. Deep down they have it in common that this THEIR Huddersfield Town won the League 3 times in a row, in grandad's lifetime.

England Scotland Wales Ireland = The Cradle of the Game

Chapter One
The Stage is Set

I called the entire collection of photographs The Homes of Football with an -s for I felt this the best title to convey the plurality of what I intended – it was and is about big & small, side by side. It also suggests roots and permanence.

Before we bring on the players and kick a ball even in anger, or amass a crowd, a ground is needed to play on. I like the idea of *sacred grounds*: places that were simply meant to become grounds, just as players were borne to become players. A bit of respect is thus due then for 'the grounds'...but of course grounds + teams + clubs are all interconnected and develop in a number of ways.

My grandfather the town mayor commissioned one such ground 'Butts Meadow' using a pool of unemployed labourers in the depression before the War. This was a communal pitch, for everyone. Years later in the same town, the team I played for, the Berkhamsted Dynamoes, finding themselves losing out in a queue, were given a farmer's spare field. At least it was our own ground now. Grounds often belonged to and were allied to branded factories, like Cooper's, a chemical company. More often now they bear the name of a sponsor that could well be a global brand.

Grounds, sacred or otherwise, have invariably evolved a unique local set of facilities, which like Doncaster's fabulously misnamed Belle Vue may be ramshackled and piecemeal yet take on the local accent and smack of this is where we are from. A criticism of new grounds built anew, in one foul swoop, is: *all very well and good but they look as if they could be anywhere.*

Topophilia (a kindly disease) is apparently the LOVE of place. Some people fall in love with a ground or even a spot within that ground and stand or sit on it through thick & thin.

After the Bradford & Hillsborough disasters, the mood of the country as a whole was suddenly appreciative: *Save the game! Do up the grounds! Save the clubs that need saving!* Which in Schindler-List style amounted to just about ALL of them. An avalanche of affection for *football back home* was brought on by the heroically failing *team-ENGLAND* at Italia'90. This was the squad of Bobby Robson and of Gary & Gazza...and featured *Gazza's tears* and Butcher's blood-red white shirt. The English part of the nation, particularly, was out of its tree with pride.

Only Manchester United had a 'museum' back then – they more than anyone got it, that football is a blood-line and grows out of its roots and mindful of your roots *just go for it!* The Premiership was now possible.

The Football Trust (for whom I photographed every new ground and stand throughout the land) picked up half the bill of renewing the game in Great Britain.

What is remarkable to a foreigner - whereas us natives might need reminding - is the amount of clubs & grounds we have in this country! And that so many have survived!! Many foreigners themselves become custodians or 'owners' of them in good times and in bad, for better or for worse.

And so my homage to our football.

This *Cradle* book starts off with a long introductory look at the sacred grounds, then the players and fans and action kicks in. There's a sortee abroad to Germany, not only holders of the best competition ever staged (World Cup 2006) but now the custodian as much as anyone of this World game and that's good reason to think of them as part of The Cradle, which is a fluid concept.

You have to move on is that popular adage. And yet, in England, with managers moving on after an average of only 10 months steering a team, history is history too soon. This reckless speed threatens to smudge the path we've come and chuck good men, clubs and reputations on the fire.

Blackburn Rovers 'Darwen End (TOIL)' 1991

Strange doings. Echoes of humble origins around Ewood; the working-class ethic ingrained.

BOLTON WANDERERS 'VIEW FROM THE STAND' 1990

Lowry meanwhile would be sat outside, painting all & sundry in shades only of ivory black, vermilion, prussian blue, yellow ochre…and flake white. Some years after his death The Professional Footballers Association bought his Burnden Park 'football painting' "Going To The Match" for a record-breaking £2million, encouraging all to look at the past amidst the rush for the present.

SHEFFIELD WEDNESDAY 'RAIN COMES DOWN' 1990

Christmas-time. Pictures of loved-ones on the mantelpiece. And here a picture of the terrace where disaster was hoisted on football-going people one sunny spring day.

BURY 'LADIES RETIRING ROOM' 1990

A place was reserved for the womenfolk to wait downstairs whilst the men watched the match from up top.

HULL CITY 'TICKET OFFICE' 1990

Hull - the embodiment of underdog & underachiever - biggest town without a top-flight football club and all that. Maybe one-day…

BLACKBURN ROVERS 'BILL FOX CHAIRMAN' 1990

The proud Chairman tells it like it is. With a bit of Blackburn embroidery. Reckons hereabouts, on Darwen Hill, football was born. The gentlemanly Godfather of football.

BURNLEY 'MIRROR MIRROR ON THE WALL' 1991

We all watched them take the League title in 1961...then slip down and down the divisions and almost out of the League entirely; almost usurped by neighbourhood minnows the Colne Valley Dynamoes. Are we not better than that?

BLACKBURN ROVERS 'THE ENTRANCE AT £4.50' 1990

That much? Oh the moans! But it use to be seven and sixpence.

York City 'Garden fence' 1991

The idea that football is a gentlemanly game where fans can be separated from each other and their feelings by sedate garden furniture is just...charming!

CUMNOCK JUNIORS 'THE AWAY ENDERS' 1996

The game is rough. It had rough beginnings and it will have rough endings and heaven forbid the tales of the living inbetween. In mining-rich Ayrshire people speak BIG about small details; they speak and swear in beautiful dialects about the game they love and the life so often cut too short to really take in.

WEST BROMWICH ALBION 'THE SINGING STAND' 1993

A new era is underway and the competition to produce the best design for the seats in the new stand, is unveiled. Happy times ahead.

BARROW 'PREPARING FOR LEAGUE STATUS' 1990

The town was a hamlet then iron-ore and shipbuilding turned it into a thriving town with a football team in The League. Then things started going in reverse. Some hang on to the notion they can cut the mustard, again.

BLACKPOOL 'LINING UP THE CORNER' 1990

Not a BIG club now. But still the big Tower and still the number one domestic holiday venue. Stanley Matthews took the play to the corners on this very turf.

Bristol City 'Meet you tonight down at Ashton gate' 1990

The midweek Cup fixture v Sunderland has a certain romance about it in an early autumn sunset; flocks of migrating birds swooping from pylon to pylon passing the red pre-fab frontage that adorns Bristol's major club..

Nottingham Forest 'Beneath the beer and blue sky' 1990

In the boozy part of the land. More breweries than lamposts.

WALSALL 'MAIN BLOCK B STAND' 1990

No one will notice if the old Fellows ground goes; they'll notice the new one if it's built slap-bang right next to the motorway. Indeed that's what we'll make of Walsall.

LEIGH RMI 'REFRESHMENT KIOSK' 2005

RMI? RMI was one of two football clubs founded at the locomotive-building works of the Lancashire and Yorkshire Railway; it was started at the main works in Horwich (where Bolton now play). The other club was started at the Newton Heath works and later became known, and famous, as Manchester United. *Show me to the bar.*

CLYDEBANK 'MOTHER & SON' 1995

Kilbowie Park hosts big Scottish names on the pitch. And off it boasts as club sponsors four local lads made good, the pop group Wet Wet Wet. One might hope there would be exciting times ahead for the comparative new kid on the block to the Scottish Football League...

ASTON VILLA 'NEW HOLTE' 1993

One of the 'original' English League clubs is having its huge standing-terrace overhauled.

MANCHESTER UNITED 'THE END OF ONE MUDBANK' 1995

The club don't have to move across town to play, as they did after War bomb damage to Old Trafford. The reconstruction work will continue whilst the team do their thing on the pitch.

MILLWALL 'OLD STYLE' 1990

Cue a husky rendition of Handbags & Gladrags for the coming of Palace.

CHELSEA 'MORE STEPS TO CLEAR' 1991

Chelsea appeal to helpers to get the matches on over the Xmas period. A thaw will undoubtedly set in anyway before then, knowing England.

Northampton Town 'Swear it's football' 1990

As if anyone could be offended by the Shire talk?

LINCOLN CITY 'TAKING THE PITCH TO THE DRY CLEANERS' 1995

Barrow 'It's behind you' 2010

(AFC) Bournemouth 'A game almost torn in two halves' 1990

The poor old mild-mannered Dean Court, with its fancy gates and leafy surrounds, is covered in spit and recrimination after the Final Day's debacle. Bournemouth are relegated and Leeds are promoted. Football gets a very bad press ahead of the World Cup.

Where the clubs are...

1 A.F.C. Bournemouth
2 AFC Wimbledon
3 Accrington Stanley
4 Aldershot Town
5 Arsenal
6 Ashbourne
7 Ashington
8 Aston Villa
9 Barnet
10 Barnsley
11 Barrow
12 Bath City
13 Bedlington Terriers
14 Berkhamsted
15 Berwick Rangers
16 Birmingham City
17 Bishop Auckland
18 Blackburn Rovers
19 Blackpool
20 Bolton Wanderers
21 Boston United
22 Bradford City
23 Bradford Park Avenue
24 Brentford
25 Brighton & Hove Albion
26 Bristol City
27 Bristol Rovers
28 Burnley
29 Burton Albion
30 Bury
31 Buxton
32 Cambridge United
33 Carlisle United
34 Charlton Athletic
35 Chelsea
36 Cheltenham Town
37 Chester City
38 Chesterfield
39 Colchester United
40 Coniston
41 Coventry City
42 Crewe Alexandra
43 Crystal Palace
44 Dagenham & Redbridge
45 Darlington
46 Derby County
47 Doncaster Rovers
48 Dorchester Town
49 Dover Athletic
50 Droylsden
51 Ebbsfleet United
52 Everton
53 Exeter City
54 F.C. Halifax Town
55 F.C.United
56 Fulham
57 Gillingham
58 Glastonbury Town
59 Grimsby Town
60 Hartlepool United
61 Hereford United
62 Huddersfield Town
63 Hull City
64 Ipswich Town
65 Kendal Town
66 Kettering Town
67 Kingstonian
68 Leeds United
69 Leicester City
70 Leigh RMI
71 Lewes
72 Leyton Orient
73 Lincoln City
74 Liverpool
75 Luton Town
76 Macclesfield Town
77 Maidstone United
78 Manchester City
79 Manchester United
80 Mansfield Town
81 Middlesbrough
82 Millwall
83 Milton Keynes Dons
84 Morecambe
85 Newcastle United
86 Northampton Town
87 Norwich City
88 Nottingham Forest
89 Notts County
90 Oldham Athletic
91 Oxford United
92 Peterborough United
93 Plymouth Argyle
94 Port Vale
95 Portsmouth
96 Preston North End
97 Queens Park Rangers
98 Reading
99 Rochdale
100 Rotherham United
101 Rushden & Diamonds
102 Scarborough Town
103 Scunthorpe United
104 Selsey
105 Sheffield
106 Sheffield United
107 Sheffield Wednesday
108 Shrewsbury Town
109 Southampton
110 Southend United
111 Stafford Rangers
112 Stockport County
113 Stoke City
114 Sunderland
115 Swindon Town
116 Torquay United
117 Tottenham Hotspur
118 Tranmere Rovers
119 Ullswater United
120 Walsall
121 Watford
122 West Bromwich Albion
123 West Ham United
124 Weymouth
125 Wigan Athletic
126 Wolverhampton Wanderers
127 Workington
128 Wycombe Wanderers
129 Yeovil Town
130 York City
131 Aberdeen
132 Airdrie United
133 Albion Rovers
134 Alloa Athletic
135 Annan Athletic
136 Arbroath
137 Auchinleck Talbot
138 Ayr United
139 Brechin City
140 Burntisland Shipyard Amateur
141 Camelon Juniors
142 Celtic
143 Clyde
144 Clydebank
145 Cowdenbeath
146 Cumnock Juniors
147 Dalbeattie Star
148 Dumbarton
149 Dundee
150 Dundee United
151 Dunfermline Athletic
152 East Fife
153 East Stirlingshire
154 Elgin City
155 Falkirk
156 Forfar Athletic
157 Glenafton Athletic
158 Greenock Morton
159 Gretna
160 Hamilton Academical
161 Heart of Midlothian
162 Hibernian
163 Huntly
164 Inverness Caledonian Thistle
165 Kilmarnock
166 Livingston
167 Montrose
168 Motherwell
169 Partick Thistle
170 Peterhead
171 Queen of The South
172 Queens Park
173 Raith Rovers
174 Rangers
175 Ross County
176 St Johnstone
177 St.Mirren
178 Stenhousemuir
179 Stirling Albion
180 Stranraer
181 Aberystwyth Town
182 Bangor City
183 Barry Town
184 Cardiff City
185 Haverfordwest County
186 Merthyr Tydfil
187 Newport County
188 Port Talbot
189 Rhyl
190 Swansea City
191 Ballymena United
192 Cliftonville
193 Coleraine
194 Crusaders
195 Derry City
196 Glenavon
197 Glentoran
198 Linfield
199 Lisburn Distillery
200 Newry City

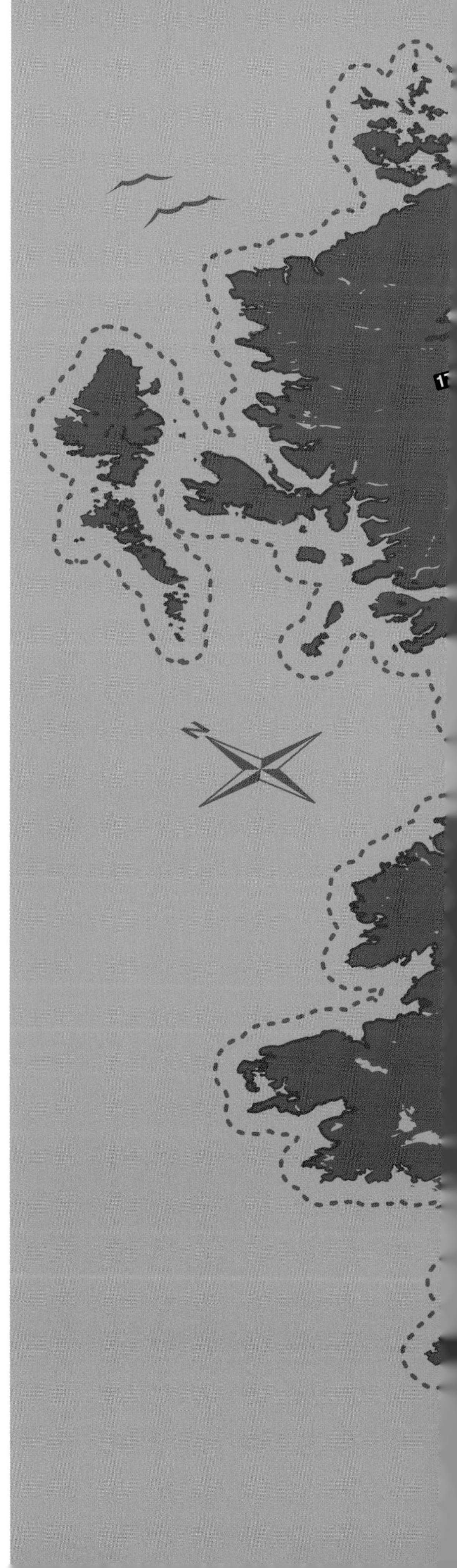

... just a handful of the clubs to grace our game!

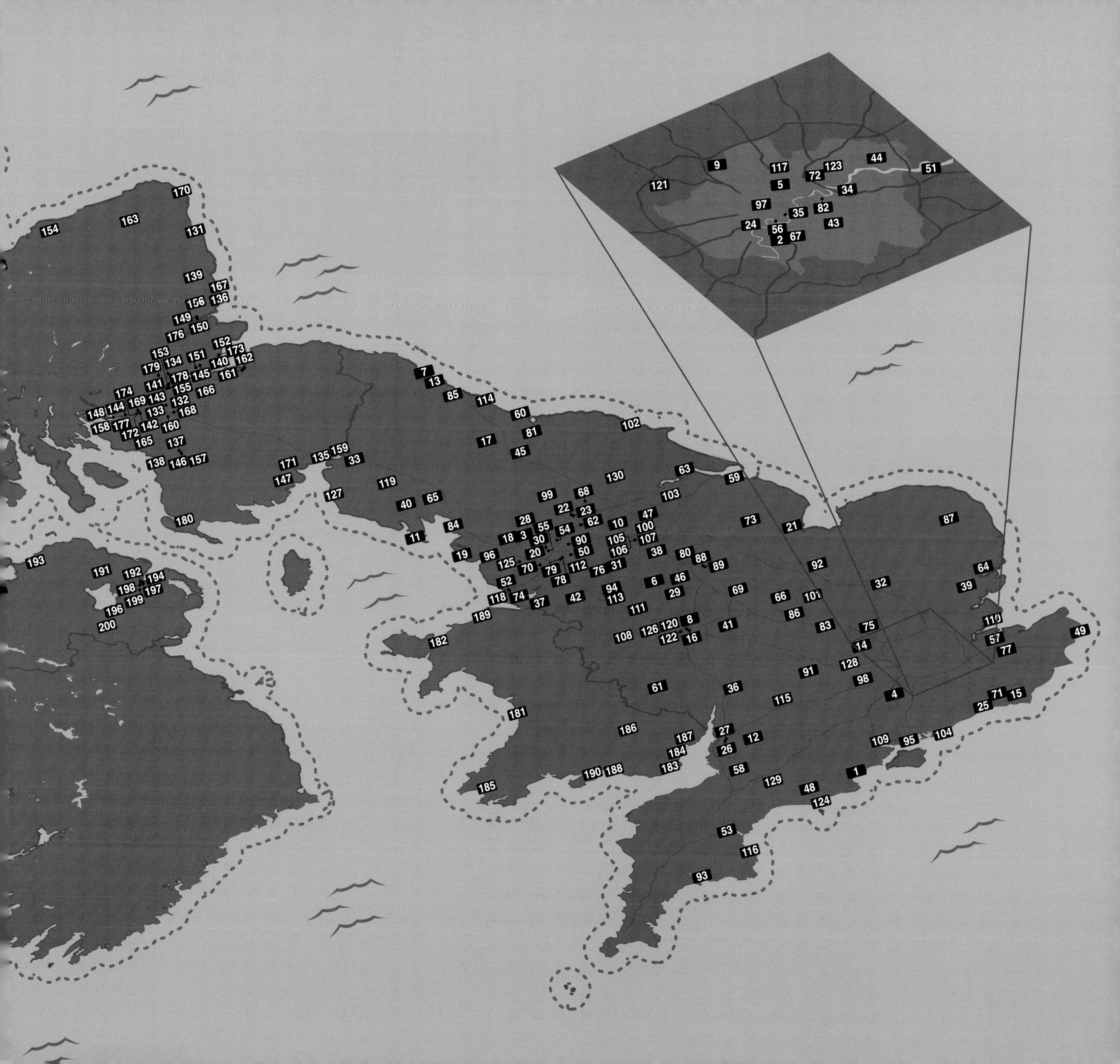
9
117
72
123
44
51
121
5
34
97
35
82
24
56
43
2
67
170
163
154
131
139
167
156
136
149
150
176
152
153
151
173
162
134
179
140
178
145
161
141
155
166
174
169
143
132
148
144
133
168
158
177
142
160
172
165
137
138
146
157
7
13
85
114
60
81
102
17
45
171
135
159
33
147
119
127
130
63
59
103
40
65
99
68
22
23
180
28
55
62
10
47
73
21
87
84
54
100
11
18
3
30
90
105
107
20
50
106
38
80
88
19
96
125
70
79
112
76
31
89
92
193
191
192
194
52
78
6
46
64
198
197
94
32
39
118
74
37
42
113
29
69
66
101
199
196
189
111
86
110
200
8
120
126
41
83
75
49
182
108
122
16
14
57
77
128
91
98
61
36
115
4
71
15
25
181
186
27
187
12
109
95
104
184
26
190
188
183
58
1
185
129
48
124
53
116
93

WOLVERHAMPTON WANDERERS 'LEEDS MUST DIE' 1990

Leeds have got a few peoples backs up along the way. Perhaps during their fall from grace. Wolves, as famous, are themselves on their knees. Someone has to be blamed.

BARNSLEY 'BLOOD RED ROAD END' 1993

In this summer recess, between seasons and amidst all the stadia (ground) improvements everywhere, Oakwell gets a soaking in blood…well, red paint in actual fact. 'This is Barnsley and we take no prisoners!' it appears to shout out. Not that the really big clubs are that bothered, just yet.

SUNDERLAND 'WELCOME TO ROKER PARK' 1990

The terrace appears quiet…then some echo.

Newcastle United 'Ever more splendid gates' 1993

SUNDERLAND 'THE ENTIRE FULWELL END' 1996

The entire end captured on film.

Ullswater United 'Patterdale panorama' 1996

Sunderland 'Building The Stadium of Light' 1997

SUNDERLAND 'CROSSING DESPERANDUM AGAIN' 2006

Sunderland, bottom of the League, could expect a win today, in the Cup, v non-League opposition.

NEWCASTLE UNITED 'THE H'AWAY THE LADS' 1990

The rum bunch of Geordies make their way to deepest Suffolk to support the lads. Who are bottom of Division Two at Easter-time.

Doncaster Rovers 'A Crack at Bellevue' 1990

Doncaster's first ground was 'the Intake Ground' where they played until August 1914 when the club went into liquidation…the ground turned into an Army base. The club reformed after World War1 at a new ground, Belle Vue. In 1997-98 the club set the record for losses in a season & went out of the League, again. The then chairman Ken Richardson was sent to prison for burning down the Main Stand.

Chapter Two

Factory Gates...Castle Gates...Where the Action is...Representing the Town

Traditionally the fans paid the players wages by their attendance so it was only right for the boys behind the desks at soccer hq to *think of the fans*. The fans don't cover the wage-bills anymore...yet in an indirect sense *they still do so* because it is the uniqueness of the British fans and the atmosphere they create in the grounds which makes the game so sponsorable and broadcastable and valuable and make it HERE where players want to play; the English Premier League is so ahead of all other leagues worldwide and the fans have helped UP its value.

Games free from money - *strictly amateur* - are valued too. But we've so come to love and embrace all that goes with the professional game that we wouldn't want to turn back the clock and do without: the badge, the numbers, the names, the backing of the towns merchants, the international sponsors, the coverage, the tv, the big business and the thing to talk about at the top table amidst the most important things.

The game would be less for people not travelling ridiculously far as near to see it, bumping into each other in service stations. Less without that intensity of having so many clubs in close proximity, and *yes, there's one near you.*

Before the day is done one gets that feeling *just have to get out of the house, out of the work-place, out of the village, out of the palace! and down the town*. That feeling is best satisfied by "going to the match".

That's where the action is.

HIBERNIAN 'AGAINST THE BACKDROP OF THE BIG TWO' 1995

Hibs v Hearts in the Edinburgh derby, with Salisbury Crags and Arthur's Seat in the background.

NORWICH CITY 'CASTLE & MOUND' 2004

The people love their city. This ancient seat plus happening football team. Promotion to the Premiership is secure and with it another opportunity for a grand homecoming. Possibly the like of which the city has never seen.

SWANSEA CITY 'THROUGH THICK AND THIN' 1994

Opponents Fulham are already relegated to the bottom division and City are left to chase mid-table respectability – a far cry from when they almost ruled the land and waved their flag in Europe.

ASHBOURNE 'THE BALL ON THE BELPER ROAD' 2005

All afternoon they watched the comings and goings, the toing and froing and pushing and pulling of the game, wherever it strayed.
And behold the derby prize, the derby outcome.

Workington 'Started on the bridge' 2009

WORKINGTON 'THE MASS FOOTBALL GAME' 2009

BELFAST 'HARLAND & WOLFF SHOT-STOPPER' 2005

On the very day George Best played in the European Cup Final for Manchester United his Dad Dickie was working a father's shift at the shipyard, overhearing the occasional news of his son's goalscoring feats amidst welding grinding crackling.

BERKHAMSTEAD LADIES 'RUNNING WITH THE BALL' 1997

Who can stop these illustrious opponents Bradford City?

GEORGE BEST 'DRIVE PAST HIS HOUSE ON THE DAY OF HIS FUNERAL' BELFAST 2005

Whether or not he was the very very best footballer ever, he certainly came from this almost ordinary street, of almost ordinary neighbours.

GEORGE BEST 'AND CO ON THE CREGAGH ROAD' BELFAST 2005

The neighbourhood produced at least 5 good footballers. But George is and was truly great. The former Wolves player, Derek dancing-shoes Dougan, has clearly upset his Protestant peers in a highly-politicised community.

GEORGE BEST 'ON THE WALL' BELFAST 2005

George is legend everywhere. These contrary parts produced him as their son.

GEORGE BEST 'PLAQUE' BELFAST 2005

The other side of this wall George grew up with his brother and sisters, Mum & Dad, an unexceptional upbringing. But something stirred inside his small person.

Liverpool 'Young mother red with pram' 2005

Liverpool have won the European Cup, to become the best town team in all of Europe. A new crown for a new generation.
We won't spoil it by saying the baby is a blue!

Liverpool 'Istanbul bound to return' 2005

The flags are up everywhere and the birds have messages on their wings with speed: Milan overhauled after half-time.

LIVERPOOL 'TWO GIRLS LEAVING THE NEWSAGENTS' 2005

Back in Liverpool they are waiting to get The Cup back. Others borrowed it for a few years.

CORK CITY 'PRODIGAL'S RETURN FRONT PAGE' 2007

Roy's homecoming, as a manager, sets the discussions racing - was he Cork's finest friend or a disgruntled prima donna? He chose nearby naval town Cobh over his home city to start his footballing career.

SUNDERLAND 'SOAKED HEAVING YOUNDBLOODS' 1991

Bottom of the League they will call on something to match the league leaders.

East Stirling 'Support from behind the goal' 1996

The fans can feel their presence felt. Which stands for something. They probably won't see a manager of the ilk of Alex Ferguson again.

KILMARNOCK 'FILING THE MATCH REPORT' 1996

Killie were a force to be reckoned with in the 1960's, Runners-Up and Champions of Scotland and 5-1 winners over Eintracht Frankfurt in the European Cup. Anyway, returning to today's game...

Manchester United 'Cantona emerges from the tunnel' 1996

Down by The Riverside, applauded by Bobby Charlton. Here he is, the champion once more…and United's star of stars amidst a strict Alex Ferguson policy of team-first.

BOBBY ROBSON 'IN THE DRESSING-ROOM' 2007

He starts by mumbling. Afterall these Gretna boys are not his team. He does not want to overstep his mark. He gives them a short story about honesty. The players are all ears. He has their respect. Bobby gets excited...This promotion-decider he tells them is about having - on the day - 7 or more players performing better than the opposition...which if you do, then you will undoubtedly win.

MIDDLESBROUGH 'BORO HOME CHAMPION ON WHINNEY BANKS' 2004

A European Cup no less is won, for the town. The boy is at his window.

FALKIRK 'HOMECOMING QUEENS' 2009

They almost beat Rangers.

HEART OF MIDLOTHIAN 'HEARTS EMBRACE' 2006

The sexiest, most unruly day in British football is the day of the THE CUP FINAL.
In Scotland, most often, but not always, Celtic and Rangers are involved. On this day Heart of Midlothian have narrowly squeezed little Gretna off the winning podium. It is Edinburgh's turn for overtly private, public shows of affection.

BLACKPOOL 'PROMOTION GATHERING' 2010

Good times.

LEWES 'THREATENING TO KISS THE REFEREE' 2007

The Sutton players are possibly spooked by playing at *The Dripping Pan!*

Raith Rovers 'Pushing for Europe' 1996

Gazza holds the ball aloft over his adversary; Brown meanwhile tries to pull down someone's shorts. Heady days; big match occasions in the realm of Kirkcaldy.

RANGERS 'GAZZA AND THE THREE GIRLS' 1996

It's not really Gazza hob-knobbing with the crowd outside Hampden, just a couple of hours before kick-off. Is it?

AYR UNITED 'MEN OF AYR' KILMARNOCK 1994

They have come from the coast for The Cup with great hope the short distance inland to the lair of their arch-rivals. And from the balcony they see their very own giant-killers slain.

KILMARNOCK 'A BEVVY OF KILLIE LASSES' 1997

Girls from factories, Saturday shop assistants. . .girls not normally to be seen at Killie matches. But their presence adds a wonderful air of innocence to the proceedings and reminds one why we bother to revere our national cup competitions.

BARNSLEY 'BOY LOOKS BACK (GOING HOME)' 1997

It's the first day in the Premiership for Barnsley. No one in all of Barnsley history has seen this before. People have cancelled foreign holidays to be here. Some live a stone's throw away. In the neighbourhood.

FC UNITED 'RETURNING TO MANCHESTER' 2010

From Buxton where they have been defeated. But generally speaking they are well on their way.

THE PREMIER LEAGUE

FOOTBALL LEAGUE : CHAMPIONSHIP

FOOTBALL LEAGUE: LEAGUE ONE

FOOTBALL LEAGUE: LEAGUE TWO

FOOTBALL CONFERENCE: NATIONAL DIVISION

FOOTBALL CONFERENCE: NORTH DIVISION
FOOTBALL CONFERENCE: SOUTH DIVISION

NORTHERN PREMIER LEAGUE: PREMIER DIVISION
SOUTHERN LEAGUE: PREMIER DIVISION
ISTHMIAN LEAGUE: PREMIER DIVISION

NORTHERN PREMIER LEAGUE : DIVISION ONE NORTH
NORTHERN PREMIER LEAGUE : DIVISION ONE SOUTH
SOUTHERN LEAGUE : DIVISION ONE CENTRAL
SOUTHERN LEAGUE : DIVISION ONE SOUTH AND WEST
ISTHMIAN LEAGUE : DIVISION ONE NORTH
ISTHMIAN LEAGUE : DIVISION ONE SOUTH

NORTH WEST COUNTIES LEAGUE : DIVISION 1
SUSSEX COUNTY LEAGUE : DIVISION 1
HELLENIC LEAGUE : PREMIER DIVISION
NORTHERN COUNTIES EAST LEAGUE : PREMIER DIVISION
UNITED COUNTIES LEAGUE : PREMIER DIVISION
KENT LEAGUE : PREMIER DIVISION
MIDLAND ALLIANCE
ESSEX SENIOR LEAGUE
EASTERN COUNTIES LEAGUE : PREMIER DIVISION
COMBINED COUNTIES LEAGUE : PREMIER DIVISION
WESTERN LEAGUE : PREMIER DIVISION
WESSEX LEAGUE : PREMIER DIVISION
SPARTAN SOUTH MIDLANDS LEAGUE : PREMIER DIVISION
NORTHERN LEAGUE : DIVISION 1

NORTH WEST COUNTIES LEAGUE : DIVISION 2
LEAGUE : FIRST DIVISION
UNITED COUNTIES LEAGUE : DIVISION 1
SUSSEX COUNTY LEAGUE : DIVISION 2
NORTHERN COUNTIES EAST LEAGUE : DIVISION 1
EASTERN COUNTIES LEAGUE : DIVISION 1
COMBINED COUNTIES LEAGUE : DIVISION 1
NORTHERN LEAGUE : DIVISION 2
KENT LEAGUE : FIRST DIVISION
HELLENIC LEAGUE : DIVISION 1 WEST
WESTERN LEAGUE : DIVISION 1
MIDLAND COMBINATION : PREMIER DIVISION
WEST MIDLANDS LEAGUE : PREMIER DIVISION
ESSEX OLYMPIAN LEAGUE : PREMIER DIVISION
WESSEX LEAGUE : DIVISION 1
SPARTAN SOUTH MIDLANDS LEAGUE : DIVISION 1
HELLENIC LEAGUE : DIVISION 1 EAST

WEST LANCASHIRE LEAGUE : PREMIER DIVISION
KENT LEAGUE : SECOND DIVISION
HUMBER PREMIER LEAGUE : PREMIER DIVISION
CAMBRIDGESHIRE FOOTBALL ASSOCIATION COUNTY LEAGUE : PREMIER DIVISION
MANCHESTER LEAGUE : PREMIER DIVISION
SUSSEX COUNTY LEAGUE : DIVISION 3
NORTHERN ALLIANCE : PREMIER DIVISION
WEST MIDLANDS LEAGUE : DIVISION ONE
WEST CHESHIRE LEAGUE : DIVISION 1
WEARSIDE LEAGUE : PREMIER DIVISION
WEST YORKSHIRE LEAGUE : PREMIER DIVISION

MANCHESTER LEAGUE : DIVISION 1
DORSET SENIOR LEAGUE
WEST SUSSEX LEAGUE : PREMIER DIVISION
BRISTOL AND SUBURBAN LEAGUE : PREMIER DIVISION
WEST CHESHIRE LEAGUE : DIVISION 2
WEST YORKSHIRE LEAGUE : 1ST DIVISION
MID SUSSEX LEAGUE
LIVERPOOL COUNTY PREMIER LEAGUE
MIDLAND COMBINATION

Chapter Three

Always Together Shoulder to Shoulder

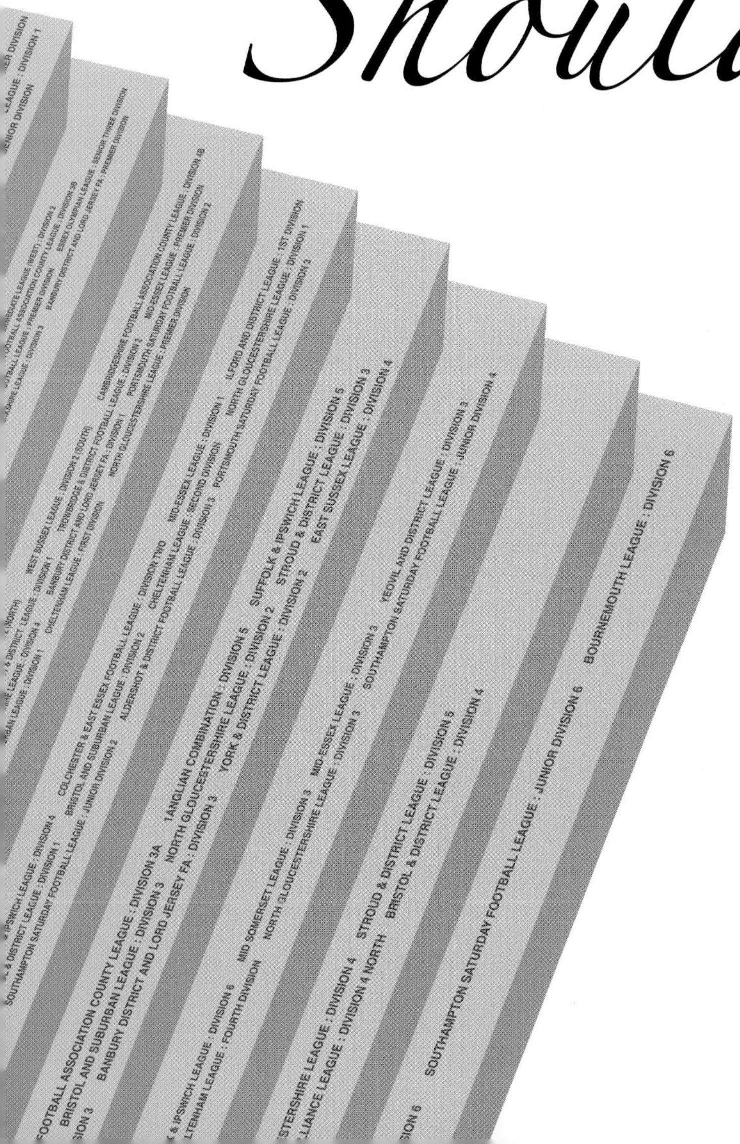

History will write: A club was borne out of the ruination of Manchester United – a ruination brought on by an American family treating it as a business acquisition, saddling it with amounts of debt that they were able to engineer through being creditable borrowers from a soon-to-be discredited banking system.

History goes on: That club was another United - FC United of Manchester. FCUM. The new United believed in club ownership by the fans; in running a club not for power nor for profit but as a club. Racking up fixtures and promotions and some defeats but nothing they could not afford to have nor to lose. Wimbledon and Ebbsfleet (formerly, symbolically, Gravesend) run along the same lines.

History goes further: Supporters Direct became the institutional arm of the fans empowerment movement.

History stands to be corrected: Manchester United were of course NOT ruined, their roots too powerful.

CARDIFF CITY 'THE TROUBLE WITH BLUEBIRDS' 1994

The Welsh side once took the FA Cup out of England. They love to play as they do, in the English League. But they will never truly settle there.

CARLISLE UNITED 'MOMENT OF SWEET SAVIOUR' 2009

In the final hour of the final match, victory over Millwall means United will not be relegated. A United renowned for 'great escapes'.

MILLWALL 'FAMILY DAY IN THE DEN' 1990

Not everyone's idea of a picnic.

SHEFFIELD WEDNESDAY 'OVER THE FENCE' 2010

Sheffield Wednesday 'On the edge of Leppings Lane' 2010

Sheffield Wednesday 'On father's knee' 1990

EVERTON 'THE PUSH FOR GWLADYS' 1990

Knowing it will then be a panic to get in, many nevertheless leave it til the very last moment to dash (from the pub).

Liverpool 'Warm flowing Kop' 1994

The legend is that there being such excitement there is no time to leave the Kop for a pee, not even during half-time. So you do it on the spot, in a paper cup or in a turn-up.

Leeds United 'Leeds hillbillies' 2008

A new generation picks up the gauntlet: this Leeds United thing. They come from over the hill, from some valley, through the bushes, avoiding spears, armed with trophies not yet awarded, or earned.

EVERTON 'TEA & CURLERS' 2009

She says she is going out this evening.

SOUTHEND UNITED 'THE CHAIRMAN & HIS SHIP' 1991

Only it's not his.

FC United 'Black dog off the shoulder' 2010

Much-loved Manchester United in some way let them down so they formed their own club…with a bedrock of 2,000 supporters. Many promotions, no debts, an increasing amount of afternoons/evenings getting-beat...offset by increasing amounts of joyous singing - including an adapted United version of Anarchy In The Uk. It's easy to wax lyrical about a new-borne; can the bairn possibly not go the way of the parent? In dreams they walk together in fields of green & gold.

Aston Villa 'Mark Weekes eyes fixed' 2006

Villa eyes are popping out of their heads at the goings-on at the olde club.

Hull City 'Staring into space' 2007

A derby encounter at Scunthorpe. The prospect of promotion to the Premiership is beginning to register in the minds of the Hull faithful. The bridge looms high and long.

CELTIC 'GO APE' 2008

V Rangers. Blood sugar high.

RANGERS 'ON THE BUS' 1996

On the way to Hampden to play Celtic for the Cup.

GREENOCK MORTON 'DROP THE DAUGHTER IN IT' 2005

Brought up with the footba'. Versus Gretna.

Falkirk 'Dancing in the streets of' 1997

LIVERPOOL 'PRAYER' 2007

EVERTON 'THE MEN ALL FIX THEIR GAZE' 2006

The match versus Arsenal is spell-binding.

Blackburn Rovers 'and City step up' Year 2000

City look for a second successive promotion...against all odds. Their fans are everywhere at Ewood Park.

McDonald's Family Enclos
BLACKBURN ROVERS BLACKBURN ROVERS
RIPPLEHEADS ICES
EUROPA CLOTHING
EIDOS EIDOS
INSURANCE
Bavaria
Nationwide
EMERGENCY EXIT
EXIT RIGHT

MANCHESTER UNITED 'CANTONA'S CORRECTIVE PENALTY' 1996

A Frenchman called Eric, with his collar turned UP in customary defiance, confines City to defeat on their own patch. Worse still...tumbling towards relegation.

UMBRO
makro

MANCHESTER CITY 'HAVE UNITED ON THE BACK FOOT' 2004

After all the years of defeats at the hands of their neighbours along with the more recent run of bad luck at the new stadium, history, today, is overturned.

Thomas Cook
Thomas Cook
Reebok
Reebok
Manchester City Football Club
mcfc.co.uk
The Colin Bell Stand
mcfc.co.uk
mcfc.co.uk
Manchester City Football Club
Thomas Cook
Thomas Cook
Euromark Menswear
Euromark Menswear

MANCHESTER CITY 'DAN & JENNY ON A DATE' 2007

The City supporters take their time to arrive properly, in good nick, for the FA Cup occasion at Hillsborough. Parking up a side street having bought some supplies for the match from a corner-shop.

HEART OF MIDLOTHIAN 'APPROACHING GRACELANDS' 2006

Actually it's a football match, The Cup Final, at downtown Glasgow's Mount Florida.

DROYLSDEN 'THE SNORKELLED SWIMMER & SPIV UNITE IN APPEAL' 2008

Almost summer. It is the very last game of the season at Stafford Rangers and with both teams already relegated the honours now are in finishing bottom or next to bottom. It is not quite clear which position is more revered...much humour envelopes the fixture and its fans.

Chapter Four

Do you actually watch the game

That we in British grounds as observers are so-close to the action as to almost become part of it (without moats & barbed-wire) in itself makes OUR game so special & intense.

Yet for at least half the match *down at the Vicarage*, at Watford, as a boy taking it all in, I would be watching the crowd - which are at least as interesting as the action - prompting my father to ask the question of me…

Wrexham v Watford 'Saturday Afternoon Education' 1997

WATFORD V WESTHAM UNITED 'COME ON YOU HORNS' 1991

The Vicarage Road end with standing area, even under the old new scoreboard.

Coniston 'Last jump of the Summer' 1991

Enjoy it whilst it lasts. Winter can be long and harsh and the games abandoned.

DERBY COUNTY 'PLAYER CROSSES THE BALL' 1992

The crowd looks on, in close proximity.

STOKE CITY V PORT VALE 'PULLING THE BALL BACK FROM THE CROWD' 1997

A final derby at Victoria Ground before it is consigned to history.

HEART OF MIDLOTHIAN 'DAZZLING THE CROWD' 1993

Versus Dundee at Tynecastle.

Aberdeen 'Celtic green the underbar' 1996

The famous old Champions host Glasgow's underachievers in what looks like a stalemate at a brimming Pittodrie.

Celtic 'Six-footed tackle' Hampden Park 1996

It takes three men to get the ball from Rangers' Gazza. Even captain Paul McStay has to get involved.

GRETNA 'A SHOT OVER THE CONTENDERS' 2005

New names in football: Gretna & Peterhead; two teams from either end of the land; emerging as the top two in this Third Division. Gretna state their authority with a pummeling 6-1.

TOTTENHAM HOTSPUR 'A CLOSE EYE ON THE FINAL APPROACH' 1999

Decisions and moves that shape a season are forged in seconds split. Ever under scrutiny from infallible technology. Versus Coventry City.

SUNDERLAND VERSUS NEWCASTLE UNITED 'A HAND ACROSS THE RIVALRY' 2007

Would they really, without policing, rip each other to bits? See how we police ourselves...we don't do high fences, barbed-wire, moats. Rather than pen us in, we would rather keep the two sets of fans apart – and not too far at that - using a human constraint; we would rather try and diffuse too much excitement and rivalry with humour, firstly.

MANCHESTER CITY 'SOAP & WATER' 2002

The orderly new Kippax takes in V.Manchester United.

Manchester United 'Sending it back to where it came from' 1992

United faithful give the ALL-SEATER legislation the red card, at Coventry, which had been the first club in England to try it back in 1981. It hadn't worked that time around.

READING 'HAVING A GO AT UNITED' 1996

An early kick-off to suit the tv scheduling.

Kaiserslautern 'Kop in chant' 2006

Germany, through their clubs & their Bundesliga have taken on many British football traditions and dressed them up as their own! Kaiserlautern's rendition of You'll Never Walk Alone is becoming the best there is.

PIRMASENS 'MODEL TEAM LINE-UP' 2006

The small German club on the French border look to their English peers for team tactics.

SUNDAY 2nd DECEMBER
PFA Centenary
Gala Dinner
To be held at
Adult
npower FOOTBALL LEAGUE
CARLISLE UNITED F.C.
V
Huddersfield Town
Carling Cup Round One
Tuesday 10 Aug, 2010
Stand: Director
Row: C
ENGLAND
PHOTOGRAPHERS PASS
LIVERPOOL
v MANCHESTER
BARCLAYS PREMIER LE
Sunday 16 December 20
Kick Off 1.30pm
YOU'LL NEVER WALK ALONE
LIVERPOOL FOOTBALL CLUB
EST 1892
MANCHESTER UNITED
ADMIT TO:
PHOTOGRAPHER
Please permit Bearer access to the above sections of the Anfield Stadium, Liverpool FC, Anfield Road, Liverpool L4 0TH. Tel 0151 263 2361, Fax 0151 260 8813. Issued subject to the rules and regulations of the Football Association Limited, FA Premier League Limited and Liverpool Football Club Ground Regulations.
FOOTBALL LEGENDS
BOBBY MOORE 1941-1993
25
Bury Football Club
PHOTOGRAPHER/CAMERA CREW PASS
Admit to Pitchside
Thro'
Reception Door 2
1998
PORTSMOUTH FC
PHOTO
POMPEY
DATE
This Pass is
SHEFFIELD WEDNESDAY FC LTD.
ADMIT BEARER
SHEFFIELD WEDNESDAY
Stuart Clarke
BEFORE/AFTER THE MATCH ONLY
AT ALL TIMES
25 APR 1998
ALL PARTS OF THE GROUND
EXCEPT TUNNEL AND DRESSING ROOM AREAS
NEWCASTLE UNITED
PHOTOGRAPHER
ADMIT TO PHOTOGRAPHERS ROOM AND TRACK ONLY.
SEASON 1996/97
Organisation Football Trust Photographer
Date 15 JAN 1997
Name Stuart Clarke
Reg. No. 7
BADGE TO BE WORN AT ALL TIMES
PROFESSIONAL FOOTBALLERS ASSOCIATION
Club, Hillsborough, Sh
SWFC
SHEFFIELD WEDNESDAY FOOTBALL CLUB LTD
PHOTOGRAPHER
SCUNTHORPE UNITED F
Scunthorpe v Hull
Saturday, 24 Nov 20
Kick Off 12:00
PHOTOGRAPHER
NEW CUMNOCK
Founded 1930
ATH
TURF MOOR
EAST STAND
BURNLEY F.C.
CRICKET FIELD STAND

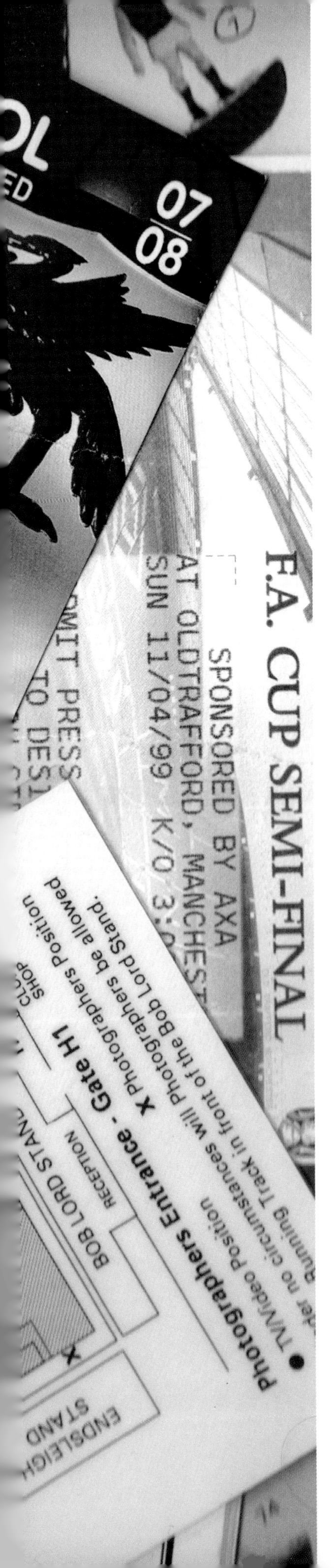

Chapter Five

Lets all meet up in the year 2000

Over the seasons we clock up thousands of grounds and matches between us. More experiences than we could ever tell-tale on. Though we'll have a go.

Finally, we seek some perspective on our lives – come summer we need a holiday from all this football-supporting: the exhaustive 10-month long test of loyalty and devotion through all weathers.

Going on a summer holiday: Let's go support England! Scotland! Wales! Northern Ireland *(they've got Sweet Caroline)*!

During the course of travels, sometimes disrupted by shoddy violent encounters, Brits have learnt to come-to-terms with would-be foes. Trips have been fantastic coming-togethers. We've most to learn from the Germans who have borrowed the king's clothes and copied his idealism…*can we have our ball back?*

'England expects...opposition' Charleroi, Euro 2000

Many of the travelling support had taken-in the battlefields of previous wars during their stay. With a win over the slightly ridiculous Germans-In-their-boxer-shorts, it is now party-time before the match with the humble Romanians.

CITIBANK

'Minding the garden' Kaiserslautern,
Germany World Cup 2006

Balls everywhere as the smallest of the German host cities turns the entire place, lock stock & barrel, into a fan fest park.

Chapter Six

Working Holiday

I expected to hate Germany, as I had done.

In all I went to 22 matches, including 27 of the 32 nations in action at all 12 venues. I saw yet more games 'live' in the big screens that complemented the Fans Fest programme (THE great success of Germany 2006). I visited neighbouring Austria, France and Belgium as well as driving 7,000 miles around Germany. I visited 3 concentration camps : Belsen, Dachau and Buchenwald as well as Luchenwald prisoner-of war camp where my RAF Uncle and 150,000 other Europeans were held until war's end. *I made friends and fell in love with Germany… and won't hear a bad word against them now.*

'England sleeping it off' Nuremberg, Germany World Cup 2006

The heat and the journeying and the emotion and the drinking conspire to lay English fans low.

‘Binoculars’ Berlin,
Germany World Cup 2006

Argentina are in town.

MEXICO 'ARRIVING ON HIS HORSE PROP' LEIPZIG,
GERMANY WORLD CUP 2006

Many many many many Mexicans are here. Their General of the Mounted Division marvels at the scene. This encounter v Argentina is to be the game of the tournament. In the best ground. The only one 'behind' the old Iron Curtain.

'English Spitfire as appropriate head dress' Nuremberg, Germany World Cup 2006

Afterall, history has it the RAF from England shot the invading Luftwaffe down.

England 'Through the Hitler display' Nuremberg, Germany World Cup 2006

All morning a trail of England fans have filed through the astonishing Museum of Terror alongside Hitler's old stomping grounds: the Parade Ground, the Zeppelin Field.

'GERMAN BOMBER' KAISERSLAUTERN,
GERMANY WORLD CUP 2006

With a World stage come to the tiny city, ever more the chance to show off.

‘English rose is prepared to strip’ Frankfurt, Germany World Cup 2006

The lassie holds sway. She has the fountain boys - and the entire crowd gathered in the square – at her fingertips.

'POOR INNOCENT UNSUSPECTING FAN GOES THROUGH IT' BERLIN, GERMANY WORLD CUP 2006

Germany will overcome the Argentinian team-of-all-the-talents. Eventually.

'Iranian couple after the Mexican rout' Nuremberg, Germany World Cup 2006

Although it's only their first game in the first round, the Iranians are shell-shocked at their Mexican examination. Their own brash, dazzling, attacking style, simply snuffed out by Marquez and co.

ENGLAND 'TWO BEERS V TRINIDAD' NUREMBERG, GERMANY WORLD CUP 2006

At least the beer is good. Here where Hitler raised his arms - all forgotten today.

FRANKFURT
YAHOO!
Continental
Fly Emirates
HYUNDAI
McDonald's
Coca-Cola
MasterCard
AVAYA
PHILIPS
Gillette
FUJIFILM
TOSHIBA
Yello Strom
Fly Emirates
adidas
AVAYA

'England kick off the campaign v Paraguay' Frankfurt, Germany World Cup 2006

The line-up under the giant spider shadow with the curious screens…

'GERMAN FILMS THE HISTORY IN THE MAKING' BERLIN, WORLD CUP 2006

He moves through the crowd.

Bergen-Belsen 'Anne Frank and others were here', Germany 2006

The sisters lie side by side, somewhere in these grounds. A billion miles from home.
It was almost summer and the end of the War when they eventually fell victim.

‘LITTLE GERMAN FAN WILL REMEMBER THIS’ STUTTGART, GERMANY WORLD CUP 2006

When they say where were you? in 20 years time, the boy, perhaps with children of his own, may be reminded of a great summer.

'A TILT TO THE WORLD' MUNICH,
GERMANY WORLD CUP 2006

The hosts have staged all manner of events and artistic treats to keep the fans interested. As if the football itself is not enough.

'NOT COVERING UP THE STATUES' BERLIN,
GERMANY WORLD CUP 2006

There had been calls for the infamous 'Nazi' statues to be covered up. The fans just work around their feet.

Ghana 'Discusses plans to seize the cup' Dortmund, Germany World Cup 2006

Yes they have to knock out Brazil to do it…but these Africans look impressive. What could go wrong?

‘Ecuador women with low cut’ Stuttgart,
Germany World Cup 2006

There is a small contingent from Ecuador, one of the less-fancied countries up for The Cup. They are surrounded by English at every turn.

England 'Phoning a friend in the heat before kick-off' Stuttgart, Germany World Cup 2006

Before a coming together with those increasingly fancied Ecuadorians.

'FRANCE PULLS OUT ANOTHER PERFORMANCE' HANOVER, GERMANY WORLD CUP 2006

Everyone thought France were going home (early). Not this time. Touché.

‘ENGLAND GLAD ALL OVER ROLLS ROYCE’,
GERMANY WORLD CUP 2006

Heading home, leaving Germany, due west, back to the island of England. Laid out on the back seat. Knocked out by Portugal. Again.
Drive on, Parker.

'Supporting mother with son in the foreground' Berlin, Germany World Cup 2006

She remembers a Germany divided.

‘Supporting son with mother in the background’ Berlin,
Germany World Cup 2006

He sees a brave new Germany.

'Hands high for the Finalists' Berlin,
Germany World Cup 2006

France v Italy. It has come to these two. Yet Germany the nation-reborn can rightly feel it is their own Final.

TOSHIBA
FUJIFILM
Gillette
PHILIPS
AVAYA
FIFA
Coca-Cola

ENGLAND 'BLAIR & FRIENDS LEAVE THE STAGE' GELSENKIRCHEN, GERMANY WORLD CUP 2006

As ever England excel at self parody. The masks also hide the faces. The defeat by Portugal.

ENGLAND 'BLOOD-STAINED BUTCHER' GLASTONBURY FESTIVAL, DURING WORLD CUP 2010

It's only Wednesday at the weekend festival but there is a huge crowd waiting on Glastonbury hill with the weight of history and expectation upon them.

England 'On a festival prayer' Glastonbury Festival,
During World Cup 2010

With masterly organisation, two massive fields at either end of the festival site have been laid on to cope with 100,000 festival-goers wanting to watch England's fate at the feet of Germany.

England 'Bunting for the hero England' Blackpool,
During World Cup 2010

England 'Tear from a window' Glastonbury,
During World Cup 2010

Chapter Seven

Auld Lang Syne Lament

When one door closes another opens and possibly vice-versa. In accepting many new things in football, including a flux of foreign players, managers, technological evidence, Adidas footballs and even German ideals *(danke schön)*, *et cetera…*we could throw our own baby out with the bathwater.

We could, for instance, start slighting Scottish football (which is the temptation when saying they can't join us in the English League). Gone already is that sense of shared experience brought about by everyone kicking off at 3pm - though this still happens on the 38th game.

The 39th parallel is surely that *auld acquaintance should not be forgot.*

'SOMEWHERE IN NORTH DERBYSHIRE 'TWO LADS' 1998

In front of the smelting plant the team-mates in their sassy kit celebrate with high fives. Dads watching.

GLENAFTON ATHLETIC 'BEVVY OF SUBSTITUTES ALL READY FOR TALBOT' 2010

This could get physical.

HARTLEPOOL UNITED 'BETWIXT BANNANA-SKINS SYNDROME' 2010

He has been named as caretaker manager. To acquire a string of wins and he will almost certainly get the top job full-time; 3 or so back to back defeats and he's out on the street. He's had roughly 15 clubs in as many years - despite Bobby Robson once naming him as probably the best coach in England. It's tough at the top. Can his players repay any faith he puts in them?

GRETNA '...ON HIS DREAM NIGHTMARE DAY' 2007

The rookie manager reflects. His charges blew a 12 point lead and took it right to the last game - indeed to the last minute of the last game - but they HAVE got Promotion, to the Scottish Premiership, today, at Ross County. The celebratory bus-ride home passes through the dark mountain surrounds of Aviemore. Springsteen's One Step Up And Two Steps Back is playing on the i-Pod.

GRETNA 'THE MAN HAS LEFT HIS MISSION' 2008

Brooks Mileson, the man with a thousand rescue-animals in his backgarden, took on the stray Gretna FC. With his enthusiasm the club ripped through the Scottish League divisions. But it proves all too much for him when they reach the highest level of the podium.

WYCOMBE WANDERERS 'GATES OF THE NEW ADAMS PARK' 1992

These are actually the old gates brought with the club when they moved from the former ground Loakes Park. Symbolic. Today's wintry queue is for a glamorous FA Cup encounter.

PRESTON NORTH END 'THE LONG ALLEYWAY' YEAR 2000

Aside an historic club.

PRESTON NORTH END 'THE KOP END RECALLED' 1996

The year of Football's Coming Home. The PNE ground is knackered and the once peerless club laid low in the Leagues. Yet the old Spion Kop is about to be redeveloped as The Bob Shankly Stand containing The National Football Museum; the Northern club-with-the-insignia-of-lamb-with-a-halo-and-crucifix are edging their way back to a promised land they helped invent.

Barrow 'On the edge' 2010

YEOVIL TOWN 'RIPPED UP OLD SLOPE' 1990

Giant-killing showground in its day. Became a superstore probably, once the club had moved to a new facility.

ARSENAL 'WRIGHT ONE-TWO' 1994

Highbury. The Clock Stand. The Gunners moving forward from the back five with a tight passing-game…against a Newcastle United poised for a counter-attack. Who shall win?

CHESTER CITY 'RIGHT PLACE WRONG TIME' 1990

Sealand Road, home of many years is no more; the ground overrun with weeds. Chester City are homeless, playing their matches at Macclesfield down the road. The lowest point in Chester's history…

Crystal Palace 'Burst through the palace gates' 1994

FULHAM 'STANDING IN THE SHADOWS' 1990

BOLTON WANDERERS 'CANTEEN GIRLS STAY BEHIND', YEAR 2000

Supping up the atmosphere, there is still a waft of the old era about the brand spanking new Reebok Stadium. But it is downstairs, almost out of sight.

Buxton 'Home supporter' 2010

Watching the fancy-dans FC United.

SOUTHEND UNITED 'WINTER'S DATE AT ROOTS HALL' 1991

The football is the place for a courting. He says.

Newcastle United 'Toon couple kissing outside the palace' 2009

During, or around, the reign of King Kev.

Heart of Midlothian 'In the shop window' 2007

A special club with a special name and connotation.

Carlisle United 'That Carlisle jump' 2007

The club specializes in famous last kicks of the game. Don't leave early.

Heart of Midlothian 'Bogs overspill' 1993

The sweet smell of the neighbouring brewery is everywhere around Tynecastle.

COVENTRY CITY 'WAITING FOR THE PLAY TO UNFOLD' 1992

Versus Manchester United at a capacity Highfield Road.

Blackpool 'The Tower with a new flag' 2010

Unbelievably, the favourite old seaside town has made it to the Premier League of the footballing World. The manager climbed the Tower and put the flag there himself.

Queen of the South 'The reward at Gretna' 2007

Getting their own back on their near neighbours: getting one over the pretenders to the Dumfrieshire throne; who humiliated them back at Palmerston in the winter.

Index of images

www.homesoffootball.co.uk

Rocking The Cradle *by Stuart Roy Clarke*

Not so much as an afterthought, rather to consider what happens before I even come to take a photograph, I want here to explain something more about the authorship process...

Gordon Taylor at book's start kindly comments on my capturing *the heart & soul of the game* and of course I would not want to argue with this commendation from a man I admire. In a Stuart Clarke arm wrestle, which would win, be the greater pull, Photography or Football?

The Professional Footballers Association which have been representing the players of the game for over 100 years have supported me for the last 20 knowing that in a sense I am one of theirs: a player. If not a player: 'a football man'. Someone who understands the game/was baptized in it.

So, what of my footballing pedigree?

It's humble. I played throughout my youth, teens, until 27 when, representing Coniston at Shepherdsbridge ground, I gave it up for The Homes of Football (a kind of national team).

Whilst growing up, my father organised youth football teams as well as entire competitions which allowed me to witness close-up, across the board and beyond my own team-interest, the way a league-structure worked...how it held together... threatened to pull apart.

I loathed some of the people who caused trouble purely for attention or to get their cheating way ahead of others. I heard my Dad on the phone trying to sort out all manner of problems; my brother and I waited patiently to hear the latest results and League tables - relayed only by phone back then. Ember Echoes, Atlas Copco, Garston, Mill End: these were great names, big teams to a West Hertfordshire boy.

Come season's end, my father dished out medals and cups in his various roles and why he did it in the first place was to make people feel a part of something bigger. He loathed religion: this was his. I took up this ethos quite naturally in the way I approached The Homes of Football. Plural.

To get to the heart & soul of football in my style I have to mine the *innards* and I have to explore the outer limits. Like a sheepdog I round up things, make sure nothing escapes. Like a surgeon I have to delve and look and poke with my eye everything around the epicentre of the arousal. The arousal is foot-ball.

I jump on the back of the teams and the occasions which are pumping blood and oxygen through the game. I want their excitement.

I also get curious about those clubs on the point of inclusion, expulsion, relegation, liquidation, re-invention. Something slightly porno in this bit and if you look at the cover picture "A Crack At BelleVue" it has that sense of peeking at something that perhaps we should not be seeing, or not be seeing on our own, or not be seeing on its own.

There is a great plurality about what I do.

I first went to Northern Ireland back in the 1980's; Derry's Bogside as well as the capital Belfast were imposing and dangerous places. Best avoided. And yet it's kind of turned around; nowadays the troubles and the terrifying graffiti (their visual legacy) are treated as art works and for tourists to hop off the bus and admire.

What amazed me with my own interest is how a place – Northern Ireland - so damaged, could produce superlatives: the BEST footballer AND the best singer? not quite the same person but in fact George Best and Van Morrison were borne within a mile of each other, 9 months apart, their fathers both working in the Harland & Wolff Shipyard. How did the genie manage to get out of this particular bottle? What was in the water?

Who knows where 'a best' could emerge? It could be a club providing an experience like no other? It could be just the one game where the lucky attendee can say *I was there.*

Whether a football-home did or did not produce anything much in the past, who knows in the future just what it might turn up?

Right out on the edge of the Kingdom if not falling off, Derry City's is an extraordinary journey and trial: over time this has meant the football club going into exile 30 miles away to play in a rival's town (Coleraine), withdrawing from all leagues, being accepted south of the border into the League of Ireland, tasting European competition, being thrown out the league for financial fiddling, reinstated then automatically demoted, arriving at the present. And tomorrow? *Watch this space!*

I am drawn to the underdogs. Even the bad boys made good. This anti-hero worship is a typically British trait. There was something thrilling about Millwall's Old Den as there was with the old Upton Park. I remember going there as a Watford fan and having to keep quiet even as my boys scored. It shouldn't be like this ideally and we certainly wouldn't plan for it to be like this.

Having a *Home* ground of your own is peculiarly important in British football folklore, and the regime of 'home' and 'away' fixtures and rituals in a 9-month long season creates an intensity, a sexiness. *Home* coupled with *Away* is a reward and a trial both. You have the comfort of playing at home, possibly well-supported, then the trial of being out of your comfort zone away. In the UK youth football and Sunday football are expected to groundshare. But at the more serious and professional levels such compromise is frowned upon. We each demand OUR OWN GROUND! And so we do plan. But football is not quite straight forward.

Perhaps it would 'make sense' for clubs to share, like Sheffield Wednesday and Sheffield United, both so in need of ground improvements over the years. Had they – and if they were to in the future - then there would be no *home and away* dynamic to their derby encounters in a season. Going against tradition.

It is easy for me to wax lyrical about tradition (because there's so much of it to choose from) and I have romanticised being out of one's comfort zone in travelling away...but the cruel

reminders of how it can all go wrong are there sometimes at a turn. In Boxing Day 1990 I surrendered the warmth of the family experience, to see if I could do 3 matches on one day. Or was it four? Staggered kick-offs anyhows. Racking up to the first one, weather deteriorating…Chesterfield v Burnley (11am kick-off) "Was Off", postponed. Expecting fluffy white snow to blanket the seven steely hills of Sheffield, I was suddenly inside, HILLSBOROUGH, game on, rain-lashed. Hardly romantic. Crushingly sad. Bad management had cost many away supporters their lives on this very spot just over a year before. Why do we do this to ourselves? I wondered. *Tradition!*

I can't criticise the people who try and push the game forward. The inventors. Personally I am probably a back-to-the-future kid, loyal to the good things he saw signposted in his youth. Not happy until those good things are returned to happy days – and the reality is they might not be.

When I was at college in the early 1980's, I began a project which to this day loans a cognitive thread throughout all three bodies of my photographic work: "The Homes of Football" / "Scenes from A British Summer Country Pop Music Festival" / "Cumbria Surrounded". That work-in-progress was entitled *Nine Lives* and had me roaming England looking at and trying to imagine in photos what it must be like growing up in different parts of the country. I so wanted to find riches everywhere.

When in 1989 I was commissioned by 20-20 magazine to adopt a similar approach in a trip to Scotland for the Wet Wet Wet story (we called it "Glasgow Reign") I was in my element. But the shoot was too soon over. I wanted to extend it to other places, other lives and certainly not just celebrity inspired.

I had then, wandering the streets (of Glasgow), come up with the shape of *The Homes of Football.*

How a thing begins is fascinating. A small part can become the stuff of local or even national legend…when I look at the hilly catchment area of the River Clyde which ends up in Glasgow, and gives Clydebank its name, I am moved to thinking of the lives of managerial greats Bill Shankly, Jock Stein and Matt Busby. And now Alex Ferguson. All borne of the Clyde.

I can't help looking at both Manchester United and Liverpool FC and thinking there is something of the Scottish Clyde in their make-up. At Old Trafford, I see to this day a tremendous rootedness, civility, fraternity. Fergie, Sir, might be thanked for this. Meanwhile, the Kop still sways to the spirit of Shankly and this can be foreboding for the opposition.

Mine own upbringing is leafier and greener. Hertfordshire-sourced.

One spring evening, end of season, Graham Taylor came to the youth presentation night, ushered by my Dad…he was being unveiled as the new Watford manager and he wanted to get stuck into the community, straight away. Even before the Press could get him. My brother and I aged 17 & 15 were the first to get to chat to him – he asked us what we liked and measure for measure what we did not like about Watford and its current crop of players. He wrote it down! He really valued our opinion. At Lincoln he had racked up a record amount of points as a rookie manager – his playing career cut-short through injury. He listened, he learnt.

Now GT is back at Watford, as chairman. And again they are doing well before a new generation of Watford supporters.

Old-schooler Ken Bates – if he was of any school - is the kind of man I think of as *Versus Stuart Clarke.* The opposition. Not someone I could ever team with. When once I was sorting out access to photograph Stamford Bridge on a match day from a promontory and was being told for no good reason by 'a secretary' that it just wasn't possible - each trying to get a word in edgeways – I was suddenly seized (over the phone) by Chairman Bates who had obviously bowled into the office looking for a bruising encounter…with anyone. He used half his swear words on me. When I see people clearing the Stamford Bridge steps of snow I find myself asking who they think they are doing it for. (And to think I myself had worn a Chelsea bobble-hat in bed as a boy!)

Teamwork and conflict and preparation and management and Ken Bates (who puts in a hell of a shift for his £1) are all part of the football thing. As is the magic and the mystery and the unpredictability, all of which I am quickly drawn towards.

Managing a team is something my brother did – I have never had a go. Additionally I have in time had a top manager live at my house so have some insight into a manager's lot at both youth and professional levels…but there must be areas you tell yourself you will not go.

To me, in doing the Homes of Football, the changing-room was an area I chose to stay out of. Therein is the player-magic-mystery being brewed up before it spills out onto the pitch. I don't really want to see them in the changing-room. The tunnel, with its reverence, will do.

As a teenager I revered 'the professional footballer' believing they alone to have some magical talents. Wingers particularly grabbed the attention…dealing with banter from the crowd whilst beating off sliding-tackles, pin-point passing to the centre-forward in the box. I believe that the wingers (goalies too) have all along helped create the special bond our game has with the fans because of this proximity, intimacy.

In mass football games the line between player and observer is crossed. Intimacy and its opposite are confused.

This rootsy scenario accounted for my daughter. It was during a series of Uppies & Downies mass football that Ava came into being. The ancient game of football is played out in a few places across the UK and notably in Cumbria at Workington. The Ashbourne version in Derbyshire (Uppards and Downards) has Royal status - Princes Charles recently attended and gave it a proper God Blimey! It does have to be seen, or played (anyone can join in), to be believed.

But it won't help any of us four win the football World Cup.

Returning from Northern Ireland one time, beside myself with excitement at my find, I wrote to Manchester United saying I had discovered a player called "Geordie" dazzling on a pitch off the Falls Road. In a match for "the unemployed"..."should be signed up". I did not get a reply.

Very few of us are good enough to become professional players and even fewer of us actually become players; a few of us become professional scouts and player-spotters. Even fewer of us reporters and photographers. A privilege not to be abused...

I was picked up off the floor: "You alright?" Erik The Norwegian goalkeeper was concerned. I was seeing stars. When I came-to Gazza was grinning. No doubt the Millwall crowd thought him clever and took him briefly for one of their own. He had singled out 'a photographer' for target practice. Bang! Knock out.

When I was photographing for a newly-formed Sky Sports at a Newcastle United training session, imposing myself on the pitch to get better pictures, I was suddenly manhandled by Bobby Robson who made it clear that no matter who we thought we were and how important it was what we were doing, there were lines that should not be crossed.

The Press runs the game; the game runs the press.

I recall an Australian girlfriend. Another photographer! She had never been to a game. Suddenly we were given a commission: her very first game would be alongside me in the trenches at Celtic v Rangers. And before that photographing around the street-bars. Finding herself swamped by Celtic fans wanting a piece of her, as she did they, she felt it timely to tell them how her father now on the other side of the World had actually grown up amongst them back in Glasgow. He and even she was truly *one of them*. Mutual admiration time then followed.

Further down the road, we were in the blue (Rangers) quarter... her father had suddenly turned blue and lived in Govan not the Gorbals. And so it went on. Her swopping sides. I feared she would get well confused and get caught out, especially in the hands of the more enquiring Rangers supporters. As it happened the police arrived waving handcuffs, truncheons, deodorant - accusing us two photographers of leading a chorus of 'The Sash' and inciting a 'race' riot.

It's important to retain a sense of humour. It is only a game. Thank goodness it's not an actual war zone. Gazza really the only sniper.

This brings me on to a final bit about the role of the photographer. I don't want to go on too much about the way I perform (I do that in the 'student' edition of this book) but a few thoughts...

Am I there to 'record' events? Or to shape them? Am I to judge others?...to corner and in a sense bully others into being in my pictures? Who are the images for? Who will see the pictures? Who will care about what they see and what they don't see? Eveyone has a camera – am I out to outdo anyone and everyone else who is the slightest bit trying to do the same? Or is mine a unique view offered and without competition? Art even?

With the football subject, as with the festival, I am taking something commonplace and commonly experienced and slightly transforming it into a new kind of language...not quite what you may have seen but conveying the feeling for it.

I want to keep this feeling. Hold it there.

If in the collecting of 'memorabilia' we could keep just the one ground as it was – and I think we should before turning it into a car park, flats, or a supermarket – I would vote for Baseball Ground (too late) or Goodison Park (still possible). This would mean it becoming a museum, with guided tours, long after the football had moved up the road to whatever new ground. The imagination would be left to run riot at all the games ever played there.

I feel football evokes as much about Great Britain as anything else – and many foreign managers such as Wenger and Mourinho say the same. As I ever more embrace the world game / see football as a force for good that we shouldn't try keep just for ourselves, I repeatedly wonder what would have become of all of this disparate, bitty, ad hoc UK football collective had the Nazis successfully invaded the UK via the railway station steps aside Dover station back then in 1940? They did not prevail.

Instead the World invaded Germany in 2006 and it was wonderful.

And now the Germans have taken on board many lessons learnt from admiring our game and applied them to its own successful model, the Bundesliga. Oh, and the national side. *Just tell us when we can have our ball back.*

Inspired by the Wet Wet Wet and that feted trip to Clydebank (Glasgow) in 1989, the year of Hillsborough, and before that my growing up in Hertfordshire, The Homes of Football has all along lived in The Lake District. An unlikely place perhaps for such a collection about what is above all an urban phenomenon. After years at Ambleside however, we are bound for Manchester, to the pyramid-looking Urbis-named six-storey glasshouse bang in its centre. Here football's past will find its future as the new National Football Museum.

The Homes of Football will give its name to the entire 3rd Floor and much of the work including The Cradle of The Game will be rolled out there from 2011. This is of great pride to me. It took years to get a national football museum in England, Wembley being passed over for Preston's Deepdale where it was until the Manchester plan was hatched. Here now in Manchester under one roof will be the biggest collection of football memorabilia and cultural artefacts anywhere in the World. All four floors which tell the unfolding story of the game will be utterly engaging and people will surely come from all over the UK and beyond.

The ball will be there. *And in years to come another of equal significance?*

FC United 'The seeing Factor' 2010

First published in The UK in 2010 by
SRC Books, England
www.homesoffootball.co.uk

Book co-produced alongside Stuart Roy Clarke by fellow-photographer John Scott (www.johnascott.com)
Map of UK and Pyramid by www.AcuteGraphics.co.uk
Printed by Clifford Press, Coventry.

The Homes of Football collection of original film transparencies is held at the National Museum of Football, Cathedral Gardens, Manchester for the education and enjoyment of the nation and for the wider visiting public.

Book Sponsored by

Front Cover: DONCASTER ROVERS 'A CRACK AT BELLEVUE' 1990 CAT.218

Back Cover: BRADFORD CITY 'YELLOW BRICK ROAD' 1992 CAT.1000